THE ULTIMATE GEORGE W.

BUSHISMS

Bush at War
(with the English Language)

Jacob Weisberg

A FIRESIDE BOOK
PUBLISHED BY SIMON & SCHUSTER
NEW YORK LONDON TORONTO SYDNEY

FIRESIDE
A Division of Simon & Schuster, Inc.
1230 Avenue of the Americas
New York, NY 10020

First Fireside trade paperback edition November 2007

FIRESIDE and colophon are registered trademarks of Simon & Schuster, Inc.

Designed by Ruth Lee-Mui

Manufactured in the United States of America

1   3   5   7   9   10   8   6   4   2

Library of Congress Cataloging-in-Publication Data
The ultimate George W. Bushisms : Bush at war (with the English language) /
[compiled by] Jacob Weisberg.
p.   cm.
"A Fireside Book."
1. Bush, George W. (George Walker), 1946- —Humor.   2. Bush, George W.
(George Walker), 1946- —Quotations.   3. Bush, George W. (George Walker), 1946- —
Language.   4. United States—Politics and government—2001—Humor.
5. United States—Politics and government—2001—Quotations, maxims, etc.
I. Weisberg, Jacob.   II. Bush, George W. (George Walker), 1946- .
E903.3.U45 2007
973.931092—dc22
2007023723

For information about special discounts for bulk purchases, please contact
Simon & Schuster Special Sales at 1-800-456-6798 or business@simonandschuster.com.

ISBN-13: 978-1-4165-5058-7
ISBN-10: 1-4165-5058-5

AWASH

**"I think—tide turning—see, as I remember—
I was raised in the desert, but tides kind of—
it's easy to see a tide turn—
did I say those words?"**

—*Washington, D.C., June 14, 2006*

HECKUVA JOB

**"I'm a strong proponent of the restoration of
the wetlands, for a lot of reasons.
There's a practical reason, though,
when it comes to hurricanes:
The stronger the wetlands,
the more likely the damage of the hurricane."**

—*Discussing post-Katrina wetland improvements,
New Orleans, March 1, 2007*

THE 51ST STATE

"I think it's really important for this great state of baseball to reach out to people of all walks of life to make sure that the sport is inclusive. The best way to do it is to convince little kids how to—the beauty of playing baseball."

—*Washington, D.C., February 13, 2006*

TOP 25 ALL-TIME BUSHISMS

#25

"If this were a dictatorship, it would be a heck of a lot easier, just so long as I'm the dictator."
—*Washington, D.C., December 18, 2000*

SICK

**"One of my concerns is that the health care not
be as good as it can possibly be."**

*— On benefits provided to military personnel,
Tipp City, Ohio, April 19, 2007*

SICKER

**"And so, what General Petraeus is saying,
some early signs, still dangerous, but give me—
give my chance a plan to work."**

—Interview with Charlie Rose, April 24, 2007

BUSH AT WAR I

**"You know, when I campaigned here in 2000,
I said, I want to be a war president.
No president wants to be a war president,
but I am one."**

—*Des Moines, Iowa, October 26, 2006*

BUSH AT WAR II

"I cannot look at a mother and father of a troop in the eye and say, 'I'm sending your kid into combat, but I don't think we can achieve the objective.'"

—*Washington, D.C., July 12, 2007*

TOP 25 ALL-TIME BUSHISMS

24

"I want everybody to hear loud and clear that I'm going to be the president of everybody."
—*Washington, D.C., January 18, 2001*

EXTENUATING CIRCUMSTANCES

"I mean, there was a serious international
effort to say to Saddam Hussein,
you're a threat. And the 9/11 attacks
extenuated that threat."

—*Philadelphia, December 12, 2005*

THE CHALLENGE

"You know, one of the hardest parts of my job is to connect Iraq to the war on terror."

—*Interview with CBS News, Washington, D.C., September 6, 2006*

TOP 25 ALL-TIME BUSHISMS

#23

"I want to thank you for taking time out of your day to come and witness my hanging."
—*At the dedication of his portrait, Austin, Texas, January 4, 2002*

WELCOME WAGON

"I think we are welcomed.
But it was not a peaceful welcome."

—On the reception of American forces in Iraq, Philadelphia,
December 12, 2005

THEM VS. US

"Iraq is a very important part of securing the homeland, and it's a very important part of helping change the Middle East into a part of the world that will not serve as a threat to the civilized world, to people like— or to the developed world, to people like— in the United States."

—*Washington, D.C., April 3, 2007*

MORTALITY I

**"There are some similarities, of course—
death is terrible."**

—*On comparisons between the wars in
Vietnam and Iraq, Tipp City, Ohio,
April 19, 2007*

MORTALITY II

"Make no mistake about it, I understand how tough it is, sir. I talk to families who die."

—*Speaking to reporters on facing the challenges of war, Washington, D.C., December 7, 2006*

THE ENEMY I

"After the bombing, most Iraqis saw what the perpetuators of this attack were trying to do."

—On the bombing of the Golden Mosque of Samarra in Iraq, March 13, 2006, Washington, D.C.

#22

"I'm also not very analytical. You know I don't spend a lot of time thinking about myself, about why I do things."

—Aboard Air Force One, June 4, 2003

THE ENEMY II

"No question that the enemy has tried to spread sectarian violence. They use violence as a tool to do that."

—*Washington, D.C., March 22, 2006*

THE OCCUPATION

"Some call this civil war;
others call it emergency—
I call it pure evil."

—*Washington, D.C., March 28, 2007*

THE PULLOUT

"I strongly believe what we're doing is
the right thing. If I didn't believe it—
I'm going to repeat what I said before—
I'd pull the troops out,
nor if I believed we could win,
I would pull the troops out."

—*Charlotte, North Carolina, April 6, 2006*

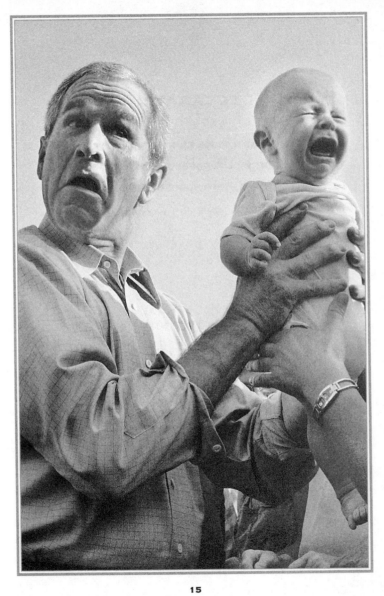

DECLARATION

**"He was a state sponsor of terror.
In other words, the government had declared,
you are a state sponsor of terror."**

—*On Saddam Hussein, Manhattan, Kansas, January 23, 2006*

TOP 25 ALL-TIME BUSHISMS

#21

**"Arbolist.... Look up the word.
I don't know, maybe I made it
up. Anyway, it's an arbo-tree-ist,
somebody who knows about trees."**
—*Crawford, Texas, as quoted in* USA Today,
August 21, 2001

SUICIDING I

"Suiciders are willing to kill innocent life in order to send the projection that this is an impossible mission."

—*Washington, D.C., April 3, 2007*

SUICIDING II

"I was not pleased that Hamas has refused to announce its desire to destroy Israel."

—*Washington, D.C., May 4, 2006*

INSECURITY

"People don't need to worry about security. This deal wouldn't go forward if we were concerned about the security for the United States of America."

—Discussing a plan to hand over security of American ports to a company operated by the United Arab Emirates, Washington, D.C., February 23, 2006

TRUE

"If you found somebody that had information about an attack on America, you'd want to know as best as we can to find out what the facts are."

—*Philadelphia, December 12, 2005*

TRUER

"You see, not only did the attacks help accelerate a recession, the attacks reminded us that we are at war."

—*Washington, D.C., June 8, 2005*

TRUEST

**"If the Iranians were to have a nuclear weapon,
they could proliferate."**

—*Washington, D.C., March 21, 2006*

#20

**"There's an old saying in Tennessee—
I know it's in Texas, probably in
Tennessee—that says, fool me once,
shame on—shame on you. Fool me—
you can't get fooled again."**
—*Nashville, Tennessee, September 17, 2002*

22

TWILIGHT STRUGGLE

"As you can possibly see, I have an injury myself—not here at the hospital, but in combat with a cedar. I eventually won. The cedar gave me a little scratch."

—*After visiting with wounded veterans from the Amputee Care Center of Brooke Army Medical Center, San Antonio, Texas, January 1, 2006*

VICTORY

**"The only way we can win is to leave
before the job is done."**

—Greeley, Colorado, November 4, 2006

WATER

**"You took an oath to defend our flag and
our freedom, and you kept that oath
underseas and under fire."**

*—Addressing war veterans, Washington, D.C.,
January 10, 2006*

EARTH

"I'm looking forward to a good night's sleep on the soil of a friend."

—On the prospect of visiting Denmark, Washington, D.C., June 29, 2005

TOP 25 ALL-TIME BUSHISMS

#19

"I am mindful of the difference between the executive branch and the legislative branch. I assured all four of these leaders that I know the difference, and that difference is they pass the laws and I execute them."

—Washington, D.C., December 18, 2000

AIR

"That's why we are inconveniencing air traffickers, to make sure nobody is carrying weapons on airplanes."

—Discussing the continuing need for heightened airline security, Washington, D.C., April 3, 2007

WIND

"My attitude about the world changed, and I know the attitude about the world from a lot of folks here in America's attitude changed."

—Discussing the September 11 attacks, Fairfax, Virginia, April 10, 2007

FIRE

"The best way to defeat the totalitarian of hate is with an ideology of hope—an ideology of hate—excuse me—with an ideology of hope."

—Fort Benning, Georgia, January 11, 2007

TOP 25 ALL-TIME BUSHISMS

#18

"I know the human being and fish can coexist peacefully."
—Saginaw, Michigan, September 29, 2000

SKIPPING

"[I]t's a myth to think I don't know what's going on. It's a myth to think that I'm not aware that there's opinions that don't agree with mine, because I'm fully aware of that."

—*Philadelphia, December 12, 2005*

SKIMMING

"I mean, I read the newspaper. I mean, I can tell you what the headlines are. I must confess, if I think the story is, like, not a fair appraisal, I'll move on. But I know what the story's about."

—*Philadelphia, December 12, 2005*

READING

"That's George Washington, the first president, of course. The interesting thing about him is that I read three—three or four books about him last year. Isn't that interesting?"

—*Showing German newspaper reporter Kai Diekmann the Oval Office, Washington, D.C., May 5, 2006*

LISTENING

"Today I heard from some opinions that matter a lot to me, and these are the opinions of those who wear the uniform."

—*Washington, D.C., December 13, 2006*

BOOK CLUB

"And truth of the matter is, a lot of reports in Washington are never read by anybody. To show you how important this one is, I read it, and our guest read it."

—*Speaking with Prime Minister Tony Blair about the Iraq Study Group, Washington, D.C., December 7, 2006*

TOP 25 ALL-TIME BUSHISMS

17

"I think anybody who doesn't think I'm smart enough to handle the job is underestimating."
—*In* U.S. News & World Report, *April 3, 2000*

SEEING

BUSH: **Peter, are you going to ask that question with shades on?**

WALLSTEN: **I can take them off.**

BUSH: **I'm interested in the shade look, seriously.**

WALLSTEN: **All right, I'll keep it, then.**

BUSH: **For the viewers, there's no sun.**

WALLSTEN: **I guess it depends on your perspective.**

BUSH: **Touché.**

—An exchange with Los Angeles Times *reporter Peter Wallsten, who is legally blind, Washington, D.C., June 14, 2006*

DECIDER I

"My job is a job to make decisions.
I'm a decision—if the job description were,
what do you do—it's decision maker."

—Tipp City, Ohio, April 19, 2007

DECIDER II

"I'm the decider, and I decide what is best.
And what's best is for Don Rumsfeld to remain
as the secretary of defense."

—Washington, D.C., April 18, 2006

DECIDER III

"The question is, who ought to make that decision? The Congress or the commanders? And as you know, my position is clear— I'm a commander guy."

—Washington, D.C., May 2, 2007

OPTIMISM

"I think that the vice president is a person reflecting a half-glass-full mentality."

—Speaking on National Public Radio, January 29, 2007

EMBROIDERY

"I said to her, make sure the rug says 'optimistic person comes to work.'"

—Describing his instructions to the First Lady in choosing a rug for the Oval Office, Tipp City, Ohio, April 19, 2007

=== TOP 25 ALL-TIME BUSHISMS ===

#16

"See, in my line of work you got to keep repeating things over and over and over again for the truth to sink in, to kind of catapult the propaganda."
—Greece, New York, May 24, 2005

GOAL 1

"I aim to be a competitive nation."

—San Jose, California, April 21, 2006

GOAL 2

**"He's helped the World Bank recognize
that eradication of world poverty is
an important priority for the bank."**

*—Defending Paul Wolfowitz, former president of the World Bank,
which was founded in 1945 to eliminate poverty,
Washington, D.C., April 30, 2007*

GOAL 3

**"The point now is how do we work together
to achieve important goals. And one such
goal is a democracy in Germany."**

—Washington, D.C., May 5, 2006

GOALS 4

**"The goals of this country is to
enhance prosperity and peace."**

*—Speaking at the White House Conference on Global Literacy,
New York, September 18, 2006*

#15

"There's a huge trust. I see it all the time when people come up to me and say, 'I don't want you to let me down again.'"

—*Boston, October 3, 2000*

GOOD

"One thing is clear, is relations between America and Russia are good, and they're important that they be good."

—*Strelna, Russia, July 15, 2006*

BETTER

"I was going to say he's a piece of work, but that might not translate too well. Is that all right, if I call you a 'piece of work'?"

—*To Jean-Claude Juncker, prime minister of Luxembourg, Washington, D.C., June 20, 2005*

OUTSTANDING

"You're one of the outstanding leaders in a very important part of the world. I want to thank you for strategizing our discussions."

—Meeting with the prime minister of Malaysia,
New York, September 18, 2006

=== TOP 25 ALL-TIME BUSHISMS ===

#14

"It's important for us to explain to our nation that life is important. It's not only life of babies, but it's life of children living in, you know, the dark dungeons of the Internet."
—Arlington Heights, Illinois, October 24, 2000

OVERACHIEVER

"These are big achievements for this country, and the people of Bulgaria ought to be proud of the achievements that they have achieved."

—Sofia, Bulgaria, June 11, 2007

RELATIONS I

**"I've reminded the prime minister—
the American people, Mr. Prime Minister,
over the past months that it was not always
a given that the United States and America
would have a close relationship."**

*— With Japanese Prime Minister Junichiro Koizumi,
Washington, D.C., June 29, 2006*

RELATIONS II

**"As a matter of fact, I know relations
between our governments is good."**

*— On U.S.–South Korean relations,
Washington, D.C., November 8, 2005*

REVOLUTION I

"You helped our nation celebrate its bicentennial in 17— 1976."

*—To Queen Elizabeth, Washington, D.C.,
May 7, 2007*

REVOLUTION II

"More than two decades later, it is hard to imagine the Revolutionary War coming out any other way."

—Martinsburg, West Virginia, July 4, 2007

UK

**"And I want those who are questioning it
to step up and explain why all of a sudden
a Middle Eastern company is held to a different
standard than a Great British company."**

*—Defending a plan to allow a company from the United Arab
Emirates to manage ports in the United States,
aboard Air Force One, February 21, 2006*

RETRIEVER

**"I've heard he's been called Bush's poodle.
He's bigger than that."**

*—Discussing former British Prime Minister Tony Blair,
as quoted by the* Sun *newspaper, June 27, 2007*

TOGETHER

**"My relationship with this good man is where
I've been focused, and that's where
my concentration is. And I don't regret
any other aspect of it. And so I—
we filled a lot of space together."**

—On British Prime Minister Tony Blair,
Washington, D.C., May 17, 2007

FASTER

**"And I suspect that what you'll see, Toby,
is there will be a momentum, momentum will
be gathered. Houses will begat jobs,
jobs will begat houses."**

—Speaking with reporters along the Gulf Coast,
Gulfport, Mississippi, August 28, 2006

FREER

"And so when I'm talking about opening markets, I'm making sure that not only is our markets open, but somebody else's market is opened."

—*East Peoria, Illinois, January 30, 2007*

#13

"We'll let our friends be the peacekeepers and the great country called America will be the pacemakers."
—*Houston, Texas, September 6, 2000*

AMNESTY?

**"Amnesty means that you've got to pay
a price for having been here illegally,
and this bill does that."**

*—Discussing an immigration reform bill,
Washington, D.C., June 26, 2007*

INTERNATIONAL?

**"Trade is an important subject here
at Caterpillar, and the reason why is
because a lot of the product you make here,
you sell to somebody else, sell overseas to
another country. That's trade. And yet it's—
it's a topic of hot debate."**

*—Speaking to workers at the Caterpillar equipment company,
East Peoria, Illinois, January 30, 2007*

CALENDAR

"This morning my administration released the budget numbers for fiscal 2006. These budget numbers are not just estimates; these are the actual results for the fiscal year that ended February the 30th."

—Referring to the fiscal year that ended on September 30, Washington, D.C., October 11, 2006

CLUCK

**"If you've got a chicken factory,
a chicken-plucking factory, or whatever you call
them, you know what I'm talking about."**

—*Discussing the sorts of jobs many illegal immigrants perform,
Tipp City, Ohio, April 19, 2007*

PLAYER

**"One has a stronger hand when there's more
people playing your same cards."**

—*Washington, D.C., October 11, 2006*

#12

"We ought to make the pie higher."

—*Columbia, South Carolina,
February 15, 2000*

COMPETENCE I

"My thoughts are, we're going to get somebody who knows what they're talking about when it comes to rebuilding cities."

— On how the rebuilding of New Orleans might commence,
Biloxi, Mississippi, September 2, 2005

COMPETENCE II

"And, Brownie, you're doing a heck of a job."

— To FEMA director Mike Brown, who resigned ten days later amid
criticism over his job performance, Mobile, Alabama,
September 2, 2005

RUINS

**"Out of the rubbles of Trent Lott's house—
he's lost his entire house—there's going to
be a fantastic house. And I'm looking forward
to sitting on the porch."**

—Mobile, Alabama, September 2, 2005

RIBBONS

**"I can't wait to join you in the joy of welcoming
neighbors back into neighborhoods, and
small businesses up and running, and
cutting those ribbons that somebody is
creating new jobs."**

—*Poplarville, Mississippi, September 5, 2005*

SAVINGS

"So please give cash money to organizations that are directly involved in helping save lives— save the life who had been affected by Hurricane Katrina."

—Washington, D.C., September 6, 2005

TOP 25 ALL-TIME BUSHISMS

11

"Well, I think if you say you're going to do something and don't do it, that's trustworthiness."
—CNN online chat, August 30, 2000

GULF I

**"We look forward to hearing your vision,
so we can more better do our job.
That's what I'm telling you."**

—Gulfport, Mississippi, September 20, 2005

GULF II

"It's a heck of a place to bring your family."

—On New Orleans, New Orleans, Louisiana, January 12, 2006

HEALTH

"And so, on behalf of the President's Council on Physical Fitness, I say to America, get outside, take time out of your life, schedule yourself, do discipline and exercise."

—*Beltsville, Maryland, May 5, 2007*

JUSTICE

"I think it's important to bring somebody from outside the system, the judicial system, somebody that hasn't been on the bench and, therefore, there's not a lot of opinions for people to look at."

— On the nomination of Harriet Miers to the Supreme Court, Washington, D.C., October 4, 2005

TRUTH

"The best place for the facts to be done is by somebody who's spending time investigating it."

—*Expressing hope that the probe into how CIA agent Valerie Plame's identity was leaked would yield answers, Washington, D.C., July 18, 2005*

COMMUNITY

"Listen, I want to thank leaders of the—in the faith—faith-based and community-based community for being here."

—Washington, D.C., September 6, 2005

VALUES

"If people want to get to know me better, they've got to know my parents and the values my parents instilled in me, and the fact that I was raised in West Texas, in the middle of the desert, a long way away from anywhere, hardly. There's a certain set of values you learn in that experience."

—*Washington, D.C., May 5, 2006*

FAMILY

**"Wisdom and strength, and my family,
is what I'd like for you to pray for."**

—*Washington, D.C., May 2, 2007*

FARMING

"I'll be glad to talk about ranching, but I haven't seen the movie. I've heard about it. I hope you go—you know—I hope you go back to the ranch and the farm is what I'm about to say."

—*Explaining that he didn't see* Brokeback Mountain,
Manhattan, Kansas, January 23, 2006

TOP 25 ALL-TIME BUSHISMS

#8

"People say, how can I help on this war against terror? How can I fight evil? You can do so by mentoring a child; by going into a shut-in's house and say I love you."

—*Washington, D.C., September 19, 2002*

MALPRACTICE I

**"And so I'm for medical liability
at the federal level."**

*—Discussing his support of medical liability reform,
Washington, D.C., March 10, 2006*

MALPRACTICE II

"When somebody gets sued all the time, they practice more medicine than is necessary and it runs up your cost."

—On how lawsuits raise health care costs, East Peoria, Illinois, January 30, 2007

JUNK

"What I'm telling you is there's too many junk lawsuits suing too many doctors."

—Washington, D.C., May 10, 2007

HOT AIR

"There's a lot of blowhards in the political process, you know, a lot of hot-air artists, people who have got something fancy to say."

—*Washington, D.C., May 17, 2007*

CONCERN

"And my concern, David, is several."

—*Speaking to NBC reporter David Gregory,*
Washington, D.C., April 3, 2007

TOP 25 ALL-TIME BUSHISMS

#6

"One of the great things about books is sometimes there are some fantastic pictures."
—U.S. News & World Report,
January 3, 2000

5

"Rarely is the question asked:
Is our children learning?"

—*Florence, South Carolina, January 11, 2000*

DISTRUST

"And there is distrust in Washington.
I am surprised, frankly, at the amount of
distrust that exists in this town. And I'm sorry
it's the case, and I'll work hard to try
to elevate it."

—*National Public Radio, January 29, 2007*

FRIGHT

"We understand the fright that can come
when you're worried about a rocket landing
on top of your home."

—*Washington, D.C., May 17, 2007*

SPAM

**"Information is moving—you know,
nightly news is one way, of course,
but it's also moving through the blogosphere
and through the Internets."**

—Washington, D.C., May 2, 2007

AMBITION

**"And everybody wants to be loved—
not everybody, but—you run for office,
I guess you do. You never heard anybody say,
'I want to be despised, I'm running for office.'"**

—Tipp City, Ohio, April 19, 2007

4

"Too many good docs are getting out of the business. Too many OB/GYNs aren't able to practice their love with women all across the country."

—*Polar Bluff, Missouri, September 6, 2004*

CHILDREN

"Because of your work, children who once wanted to die are now preparing to live."

—Speaking at the White House summit on malaria,
December 14, 2006

FRIENDS

"I like my buddies from West Texas. I liked them when I was young, I liked them when I was middle-age, I liked them before I was president, and I like them during president, and I like them after president."

—Nashville, Tennessee, February 1, 2006

TOMORROW

"We shouldn't fear a world that is more interacted."

—Washington, D.C., June 27, 2006

THE FUTURE

"I tell people, let's don't fear the future, let's shape it."

—Omaha, Nebraska, June 7, 2006

TOP 25 ALL-TIME BUSHISMS

#3

"Neither in French nor in English nor in Mexican."

—Declining to answer reporters' questions at the Summit of the Americas, Quebec City, Canada, April 21, 2001

BREAD

"And one thing we want during this war on terror is for people to feel like their life's moving on, that they're able to make a living and send their kids to college and put more money on the table."

—The NewsHour with Jim Lehrer, *January 16, 2007*

#2

"I know how hard it is for you to put food on your family."
—*To the Chamber of Commerce, Greater Nashua, New Hampshire, January 27, 2000*

HISTORY

"You never know what your history is going to be like until long after you're gone."

—Washington, D.C., May 5, 2006

FAREWELL

"This business about graceful exit just simply has no realism to it at all."

—Amman, Jordan, November 30, 2006

#1

"Our enemies are innovative and
resourceful, and so are we.
They never stop thinking about
new ways to harm our country and
our people, and neither do we."
—*Washington, D.C., August 5, 2004*

ABOUT THE AUTHOR

Jacob Weisberg is the editor of *Slate* magazine and editor of five previous editions of *Bushisms*. He lives in New York City.

PHOTO CREDITS

AP Images: ii (top row, right), 10, 24, 32, 38, 42, 52, 55

JIM BOURG/Reuters/Landov: photo in hexagon at page tops, 15

Matthew Cavanaugh/epa/Corbis: 60

KEVIN DIETSCH/UPI/Landov: 35

LARRY DOWNING/Reuters/Landov: ii (second row), 6, 41, 69, 70, 74, 79, 80

CHIP EAST/Reuters/Landov: 72

YURI GRIPAS/Reuters/Landov: 18

FIONA HANSON/PA Photos/Landov: 48

Brooks Kraft/Corbis: ii (top row, left; bottom row, left), 64, 87

RICHARD KRAUSE/Reuters/Landov: 86

KEVIN LAMARQUE/Reuters/Landov: ii (third row), 67

SAUL LOEB/AFP/Getty Images: 83

MANDEL NGAN/AFP/Getty Images: 25

Shepard Sherbell/Corbis: 58

BRENDAN SMIALOWSKI/Bloomberg News/Landov: 80

Shawn Thew/epa/Corbis: 46

MARK WILSON/UPI/Landov: 49

ROGER L. WOLLENBERG/UPI/Landov: ii (bottom row, right), 21

Alex Wong/Getty Images: 81

JIM YOUNG/Reuters/Landov: 30, 66